Iraq

THE BRADT TRAVEL GUIDE

Karen Dabrowska

Bradt Travel Guides Ltd, UK
The Globe Pequot Press Inc, USA

First published in 2002 by Bradt Travel Guides Ltd.

Reprinted with amendments February 2003.

19 High Street, Chalfont St Peter, Bucks SL9 9QE, England
web: www.bradt-travelguides.com
Published in the USA by The Globe Pequot Press Inc, 246 Goose Lane,
PO Box 480, Guilford, Connecticut 06437-0480

British Library Cataloguing in Publication Data
A catalogue record for this book is available from the British Library

ISBN 1 84162 027 0

Photographs
Front cover Mausoleum of Imam Ali El Hadi and Imam Hassan Al Askari, Samarra
(Chris North/Sylvia Cordaiy Photo Library)
Text Geoff Hann

Illustrations Carole Vincer
Maps Steve Munns

Typeset from the author's disc by Wakewing
Printed and bound in Italy by Legoprint SpA, Trento

Authors

Born in Wellington, New Zealand, to Polish parents, **Karen Dabrowska** worked on a daily paper in New Zealand for six years before emigrating to Britain, in 1985, where she completed an MA in International Journalism. She has edited a number of magazines and newsletters dealing with the Arab world including *New Horizon* and *Al Muhajir* (English section) and has visited most Arab countries. Karen is currently London correspondent of the *Yemen Times* and Jana News Agency and contributes articles on Islamic and Middle Eastern affairs to a number of publications on a freelance basis. She is the author of *Addis Ababa: the first 100 years* and *Bahrain Briefing – the struggle for democracy (December 1994 – December 1996)*.

Her travels began with an overland tour of Nepal and India in 1980. She first visited the Middle East in 1986 when she travelled to Egypt on a camping tour. She spent some time in Jordan and the West Bank reporting on the first Palestinian uprising and her interest in the Palestinian cause also took her to Tunisia and Syria.

Her introduction to Islamic art came in Baghdad where she attended an international calligraphy festival. Her most recent trip was to Yemen where she spent some time in Hadramaut, the province of mud-brick architecture and peaceful tribes who resolve disputes through mediation with mobile phones, rather than guns.

Geoff Hann, founder/director of the adventure companies Hann Overland and Hinterland Travel, is a veteran overland traveller and adventurer who has been visiting the Middle East and Asia since the 1960s.

In the early years of the Asia overland expeditions boom during the 1970s he personally drove and led over 20 group departures from London to Kathmandu by road, many by way of Iraq, others through Afghanistan. More recently he has led small groups to various parts of India, Tibet, China, Bangladesh, Central Asia, Iran and Iraq. His love of history and taste for exploring little-known routes has caused him to travel on almost all roads in and out of Iraq, including now-closed border crossings. During the Iran–Iraq conflict (1980–88) the tourist groups he took to Iraq were often the only travellers in the country.

In October 2000, after a period of absence from the country due to the Gulf War, he renewed his archaeological/historical tours to Iraq and British tourists returned to the country. He has provided the practical travel information and many site descriptions for this guide.

Contents

LIST OF MAPS

Acknowledgements

First and foremost I would like to thank Dr Salah Al-Shaikhly who suggested I write this book. Special thanks must also go to J Maan Al Khafaji, my colleague and friend, for his inspiration, patience and encouragement.

For assistance with the section on the safe-haven I am extremely grateful to Dilshad Miran and Dr Latif Rashid. Maysaloun Faraj shared her specialist knowledge on Iraqi art with me and Yusef Al Khoei provided a penetrating insight into Shia Islam. Freelance journalist Rose George made a significant contribution to the chapter on modern Iraq.

For the benefit of their experiences in Iraq, comments on the text, and encouragement I am also extremely grateful to: Dr Dlawer Aldeen, Felicity Arbuthnot, Dr Ahmed El Dawi, Julie Davies, Fran Hazelton, Zuheir Khammas, Dr Hans-Heino Kopietz, Abduallah Muhsin, Sabah Nuri, Brenda Prince, Nazeen Rashid, Aziz Kadir Samanchi, Ali Shuaib and the staff at Jana News Agency, Halim Sibahi, Dr Saeed Shehabi, Kristin Strandenes, Riad Al Taher, Trevor Thomas and Lamia Al-Gailani Werr.

This book is dedicated to my father who gave me the courage to pursue my dreams, and to the Iraqis in London and the Middle East who have accompanied me on life's journey.

The views expressed in this guide are those of the main author, Karen Dabrowska, and do not necessarily reflect the opinions of tour operators or other contributors.

Extracts
Reprinted with permission, extracts from: Kenneth Kattan, *Mine was the Last Generation in Babylon*; Anton La Guardia, *Daily Telegraph* 2000 reportage on smuggled antiquities (© Telegraph Group Limited); Jeffrey Robinson, *The Laundrymen* (© 1996 Pennstreet Ltd, reprinted with permission by Arcade Publishing, New York); Gaston Wiet, *Baghdad: Metropolis of the Abbasid Caliphate* (Oklahoma: University of Oklahoma Press, 1971); Lorenzo Kimball, *The Changing Pattern of Political Power in Iraq, 1958–1971* (New York: Robert Speller, 1972); Freya Stark, *Baghdad Sketches* (London: John Murray, 1947); Stephen Longrigg, *The Middle East: A Social Geography* (London: Duckworth, 1963); Tore Kjeilen extract on Mandeans from *Encyclopaedia of the Orient* (internet edition); Samir Al-Khalil, *The Monument* (London: Andre Deutsch, 1991); Mrs Sue Morris quotation from Sir Mortimer Wheeler; Leonard Cottrell, *Land of the Two Rivers* (© 1963 Leonard Cottrell, the Estate of Leonard Cottrell); Yitzhak Nakash, *The Shi'is of Iraq* (© 1994 Princeton University Press); Gavin Young, *Iraq: Land of Two Rivers* (© 1980 Gavin Young, Gillon Aitken Associates).

Introduction

Iraq, the land between the two rivers, the Tigris and the Euphrates, is a jigsaw puzzle with three main pieces: the mountainous snow-clad north and northeast making up about 20% of the country, the desert representing 59% and the southern flat lowland alluvial plain making up the remainder.

The history of Iraq has often been a history of conflict and bloodshed. But during periods of serenity, splendid civilisations have emerged to make numerous indisputable contributions to the history of mankind: it is the land where writing began, where zero was introduced into mathematics and where the tales of the thousand and one nights were told. Iraq was the home of the famous Hanging Gardens of Babylon and the mythical Tower of Babel. Qurnah is reputed to be the site of the biblical Garden of Eden. Splendid mosques and palaces were built by rulers who insisted on nothing but the most magnificent. Through trade, Iraq absorbed the best of what its neighbours had to offer and incorporated the innovations of others into its own unique civilisation.

In the 20th century Arab nationalism was nourished in Iraq – it was the first independent Middle Eastern state and developed a strong Arab identity. Art was encouraged and Baghdad became the venue for many international cultural festivals. It now has the Arab world's largest museum, the Iraqi Museum, with 28 galleries. The 14m oil nationalisation mural on the road to Baghdad airport is also the largest in the Arab world. Today the capital, Baghdad, has evolved into a sprawling 20th-century metropolis on the east and west banks of the River Tigris.

At the time of writing the Iraqi people are suffering from some of the most stringent economic sanctions ever imposed by the United Nations and from life under Saddam Hussein's totalitarian regime. They are also under the threat of a massive bombardment, if the USA believes that weapons of mass destruction are being hidden or developed. But anyone who doubts that the country will emerge from this difficult period and contribute once again to all noble human endeavours does not understand Iraq's resilient nature.

In the words of Gavin Young, author of *Iraq: Land of Two Rivers*:

> if the oil should ever run out, the twin rivers will still uncoil like giant
> pythons from their lairs in High Armenia across the northern plains,
> will still edge teasingly closer near Baghdad, still sway apart lower
> down, still combine finally at the site – who knows for sure that it
> was not? – of the Garden of Eden, and flow commingled through
> silent date-forests to the Gulf.

> Whatever happens, the rivers - the life-giving twin rivers for which
> Abraham, Nebuchadnezzar, Sennacherib, Alexander the Great,
> Trajan, Harun Al Rashid and a billion other dwellers in Mesopotamia
> must have raised thanks to their gods – will continue to give life to
> other generations.

How this guide came to be written

In 1987 I had a conversation with an Iraqi gentleman who was eager to sell his country as a tourist attraction. 'It's a great place really, you can drink in the hotels.' I found it sad he was totally convinced that the presence – or absence – of alcohol was the most important consideration for Western tourists.

In 1988 the assistant editor of *Arts and the Islamic World* was invited to Baghdad for a calligraphy festival. He kindly asked the Iraqi Cultural Centre in London to make it possible for me to attend because *New Horizon* (news and views from the Muslim world), the magazine I was editing at the time, had a large cultural section.

I visited Baghdad and several other cities in Iraq and returned to London convinced that it was 'a great place': hence my resolve to learn more about the country and its people. My initial journey of discovery took me down the political road, but my first impressions of Iraq as an amazing tourist destination never left me.

This book initially began as a project proposed by Dr Salah Al-Shaikhly, the editor-in-chief of the London-based publishing company Arab Book Club Publications. I was commissioned to write a travel guide in 1997 and a great deal of work went into producing the first draft. But due to other, more urgent commitments, neither myself nor Dr Shaikhly pursued the final publication of the book.

I then discussed the project with Bradt, who are never afraid to introduce tourists to what John Simpson would describe as 'strange places, questionable people'. Both Hilary Bradt and Tricia Hayne were very supportive and encouraging. Only their unshakeable belief in the potential for tourism in a country where nothing is certain – and the practical travel information from Geoff Hann who has made several recent visits – ensured this guide became a reality.

Part One

General Information

IRAQ FACTS

Area 441,839km^2
Population 22.4 million (1997)
Location Middle East
Time GMT + 3
Electricity AC 220V
Border countries Iran, Jordan, Kuwait, Saudi Arabia, Syria, Turkey
Flag Three bands, red over white over black, with three green stars in the white band and the words *Allah u akbar* (God is Great) written in Arabic
Capital Baghdad
Climate Mild to cool winters; hot, cloudless summers
Main towns Basrah, Mosul, Kirkuk
Currency Iraqi dinars (ID = 1,000 fils)
Official language Arabic
Religion 95% Muslim; Christian minority mainly in villages around Mosul; Jewish minority mainly in Baghdad. Religious sects: Sabaeans, Yazidis
Ethnic divisions Arabs 75–80%, Kurds 15–20%, Turcoman, Assyrian or other 5%
Type of government Republic
Governorates The country is divided into 18 governorates: Nineveh, Salah ad–Din, At Ta'meem, Diala, Baghdad, Al–Anbar, Babylon, Karbala, An–Najaf, Al–Qadisiya, Al–Muthanna, Thi–Qar, Wasit, Maysan, Basrah, D'hok, Arbil, and Sulaimaniya
Head of State Saddam Hussein
Ruling party Arab Baath Socialist Party
Government Supreme power is vested in the Revolutionary Command Council (RCC), made up of members of the regional command of the Arab Baath Socialist Party
Independence October 3 1932
Communications and useful telephone numbers International dialling code for Iraq is +964
Economy State-controlled with growing private sector. Main revenue from oil and gas.
GDP US$30.4bn; per head US$1,300; growth 12.0% (1997)
Inflation 165% (1997)

Background

HISTORICAL SKETCH

The ancient name of Mesopotamia is Greek for 'land between the two rivers'. The name Iraq, meaning 'firmly rooted country', did not emerge until the 7th century in acknowledgement of the country's influence on ancient civilisations. Historians have labelled Mesopotamia as the cradle of civilisation. In 3000BC Sumerian kings, who ruled at the same time as the earliest Egyptian dynasties, developed the first civilisations. Hammurabi (1792–50BC), a ruler of Babylon, which emerged from a union of the ancient Sumerian and Akkadian kingdoms, developed one of the earliest known codes of law to ensure that 'justice prevailed in the country' and that 'the strong may not oppress the weak'. The hanging gardens of Babylon, a creation of King Nebuchadnezzar (605–562BC) are regarded as the seventh wonder of the ancient world. After Nebuchadnezzar's enlightened rule the area was conquered by a number of different invaders.

In AD637 Mesopotamia was completely subjugated by the Arabs and their new, monotheistic faith: Islam. Between AD750–1258, the era of the Abbasid caliphs (Islamic rulers), Baghdad was the intellectual centre of the Islamic world, where art, science and philosophy flourished. The writings of Aristotle and Plato were translated in the House of Wisdom and advances in medicine, astronomy and other disciplines laid the foundations for modern Western sciences.

From 1638 until World War I, Iraq was part of the Ottoman Empire governed from Istanbul. After the war, the British mandate followed and in 1932 Iraq was formally admitted to the League of Nations as an independent state governed by a constitutional monarchy installed by the British. The monarchy was overthrown in 1958 by the nationalist Free Officers in a coup led by Brigadier Abdul Karim Qasim. Qasim was murdered in 1963 during a Baathist-led coup. Nine months later the Baathists were overthrown in a counter-coup but succeeded in toppling the government for a second time in 1968. They have remained in power ever since. In a country characterised by political instability, where the government has been overthrown 23 times since 1920, the Baath Party became extremely well versed in the art of political survival.

The 1980s were dominated by the Iran–Iraq war, which left an estimated 400,000 dead and 750,000 wounded. Iraq invaded Iran in the hope of toppling the fundamentalist Islamic regime and controlling the Shatt Al Arab. It failed and was left with demands to repay foreign debts of more than US$75 billion to the countries that helped finance the war, especially Saudi Arabia and Kuwait.

The next military action came with the invasion of Kuwait on August 2 1990 prompted by Saddam Hussein's unrelenting ambition to turn Iraq into a regional superpower, his anger at Kuwaiti insistence on repayment of debts, his claim to part of the Rumaila oilfield, and his determination to secure the Kuwaiti islands of Bubiyan and Warbah. Economic sanctions were imposed as a result of the invasion. Arab and international mediation failed to persuade Iraq to withdraw and the UN authorised the use of force. On January 17 1990 a five-week bombing campaign, authorised by the United Nations and led by America, began. The bombardment left an estimated 100,000 dead and a further 300,000 wounded. In March 1991, popular uprisings in the north and south of the country, in which disenchanted members of the Iraqi army and civilians took part, were brutally crushed. United Nations Security Council Resolution (UNSCR) 688, which 'condemns the repression of the Iraqi civilian population in many parts of Iraq, including most recently in Kurdish populated areas', was invoked by Britain, France and the USA to establish a safe-haven for the Kurds in the north of the country, which is administered as an autonomous zone. Damage from the Gulf War was estimated at US$200–250 billion. In 2001, 11 years after the invasion of Kuwait, economic sanctions are still in force (see *Economy and sanctions*, page 9).

GEOGRAPHY

Except for the narrow strip of land providing access to the Persian Gulf (the Arabs call it the Arabian Gulf) known as the *Shatt Al Arab,* Iraq (441,839km², slightly larger than Sweden) is landlocked, with Iran to the east, Kuwait and Saudi Arabia to the south, Jordan and Syria to the west and Turkey to the north.

Iraq's landscape is dominated by two rivers, the **Tigris** (1,850km long, of which 1,418 are in Iraq) and the **Euphrates** (2,350km, of which 1,213 are in Iraq). The two rivers are separated from each other by 250 miles of open plain when they emerge from Turkey's Taurus mountains and flow into Iraq. The Tigris flows southwards, the Euphrates to the southeast. Near Baghdad they are separated by a mere 20 miles. At Qurnah in southern Iraq, reportedly the site of the Garden of Eden, their waters join the Shatt Al Arab.

For centuries the silt of the rivers, deposited in the valleys through which they flow, has ensured the fertility of the soil. Their waters are also essential for irrigation. Floods, most common in March, April and May, have caused serious problems for centuries, as Sumerian legends and the biblical story of the flood tell us. In 1954 Baghdad was devastated by a flood that killed thousands and resulted in an estimated US$50 million worth of damage.

Iraq is made up of the snow-clad mountains of the north and northeast (which account for 20% of the land area); the desert (59% of the land area); and the flat lowland alluvial plain in the south, famous for its unique swamps and marshlands, which have been largely destroyed due to a large-scale drainage scheme. This area was once the home of some 200,000 marsh Arabs,

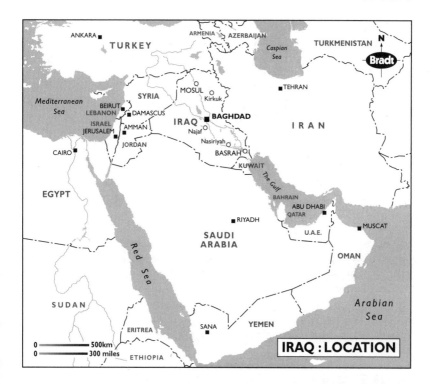

IRAQ : LOCATION

also known as *Ma'dan*, whose unique lifestyle dated back to 3000BC, the time of the Sumerians. Today very few marsh Arabs have retained their traditional way of life.

The Kurds, meanwhile, inhabit the mountainous region, with magnificent snow-clad peaks ranging from 3,000ft to more than 12,000ft near the Iranian and Turkish borders. On the lower slopes the temperate climate and plentiful rainfall make the growing of fruit, vegetables, grain and tobacco possible. The rest of the country's population is concentrated along the Tigris and Euphrates, whose waters are the lifeblood of the country.

Finally, the desert, where bedouins live off their herds of camels, goats and sheep, has been described in a geography textbook as 'an area so desolate and uninviting that even a rattlesnake would feel lonely there'.

CLIMATE

Iraq has only two seasons: hot (where temperatures can rise as high as 43°C) and cool (10°C). For visitors the best time to visit is during the seven cool months, October to April. In January the mean temperature in Baghdad is 9.4°C. Mosquitoes are abundant during the hot season. In the south they carry malaria. During the summer months, June, July and August, the country is swept by the southern and southeasterly sirocco wind and dust storms. The *shamal* is the prevailing wind from the north which dries out the air. Rainfall is high in the northern highlands but only 6in fall annually on the alluvial plain.

FLORA AND FAUNA

Finding a date is never a problem in Iraq – there are 22 million date trees in the country with 450 varieties, but only four are commercially exploited. The trunk of the date palm grows to a height of up to 18m. A female tree bears 200–1,000 dates. A cluster of dates weighs up to 12kg, and the annual yield of a single tree may reach 270kg. The tree begins to bear fruit in its eighth year, reaches maturity at 30 years, and begins to decline at about 100 years. Before sanctions were imposed in 1990 Iraq supplied over 80% of the world's dates.

The landscape determines the vegetation. Oak, pine, walnut, willow, wild vines and buttercups are found in the northern highlands. Reeds dominate the southern marshlands, where saltwort, camel thorn and box thorn are also found. For short periods in the spring the desert blooms provide sheep, goats and camels with spear grass, rock rose, saltbushes and other plants. Orange and lemon trees are grown extensively in the shade of millions of date palms in the centre and south of the country. Wheat and barley are grown in northwest Iraq between the Tigris and Euphrates, and vast areas of rice fields have been planted in the south.

The most fertile region is found on the banks of the Tigris and Euphrates where a network of irrigation ditches directs water to farmland. About 50% of the land is arable but only 13% is under cultivation. Agricultural products include wheat, barley, and fruits such as apples, olives, grapes, pears, oranges and pomegranates.

The livestock industry is concentrated around sheep, cattle, goats and poultry. The country is also a centre for breeding the Arabian horse.

Conservation has not been a priority in Iraq. The oryx, ostrich and wild ass have practically been wiped out. The last lion was killed in 1910. During the 1950s gazelles were hunted from cars with drastic consequences. Bats, rats of various species, jackals and wildcats are the most common mammals, with wild pig and gazelle found in remoter parts. Reptiles are numerous and include lizards, snakes, and tortoises. Otters were once found in the marshes and streams as were fish, mainly from the carp family.

There is a distinct hierarchy among the birds: eagles, vultures, kites and other birds of prey make a meal of smaller birds. Water birds include pelicans, geese, ducks and herons. Storks are a common sight throughout the country. They build their nests on trees, roofs and domes.

The hoopoe is a legendary creature who sheltered the Prophet Mohammed with its wings when he fell asleep in the desert. In gratitude the bird was offered a gift and the vain creature chose its glorious crown. The sand grouse, which resembles a pigeon, nests in the desert in temperatures of over 100°F. Water is brought to the young on the breast feathers of their parents who shelter them with their wings.

Migrating waterfowl wintering in the marshes of southern Iraq have become a favourite target for poachers, who sell them as a cheap alternative to poultry in Iraq's sanctions-hit markets. The birds, which arrive annually by the thousand from Siberia, Scandinavia or China, once faced only a few amateur hunters interested in their exotic winter plumage. Today, poachers eagerly await their arrival and wild ducks, moorhens and greenfinches also end up in the cooking pot. Between 20,000 and 30,000 migratory birds are sold each season in Baghdad's markets. The feathers are used for stuffing chair cushions and mattresses.

POPULATION

Iraq has a population of 22.4 million (1997 census) with around 30% engaged in agriculture. The rural–urban drift began in the 1920s after oil was discovered, and increased during the 1970s, at the peak of the oil boom. The development of an oil-based economy and urban society brought about significant changes to the social structure as the traditional authority of tribal sheikhs diminished. But, as in all Arab societies, the elders are still respected and the influence of religious leaders is evident. Seventy–five percent of the people now live in towns. Between 1960 and 1992 the urban population increased by 5.2% per year. The Iraqis have an unquenchable thirst for knowledge and the country is said to have the highest number of PhD holders in the world. An estimated five million Iraqis are living abroad as expatriates or political refugees.

GOVERNMENT

Political power in Iraq is dominated by Saddam Hussein (president since 1979), his family, especially his two sons Uday and Qusay, members of his Tikriti clan and a number of senior Baath Party members. The only legal political party, the Arab Baath Socialist Party, with a pan-Arab ideology focusing on unity, freedom and socialism, has become a medium for the distribution of patronage. The regime's control is maintained by a brutally efficient security apparatus. The main opposition parties inside Iraq which operate clandestinely are the Iraqi Communist Party, the Dawa Party and the Supreme Council of the Islamic Revolution in Iraq. There are over 80 Iraqi opposition parties in exile.

GOVERNORATES

(Population figures based on 1998 estimates)

Baghdad	6,932,552	Qadissiya	700,812
Nineveh	1,807,784	Wasit	643,371
Basrah	1,746,618	Najaf	640,487
Babylon	1,024,571	Salaheddin	600,896
Thiqar	1,003,332	Maisan	537,735
Diyala	837,332	Kerbala	441,286
Al–Tamim	839,571	Muthanna	350,644
Anbar	823,368		

The following governorates in the safe-haven in the north are administered by the Kurds and are not under the control of the government in Baghdad:

Sulaimaniyah	1,300,828	Dohuk	482,261
Arbil	1,096,899		

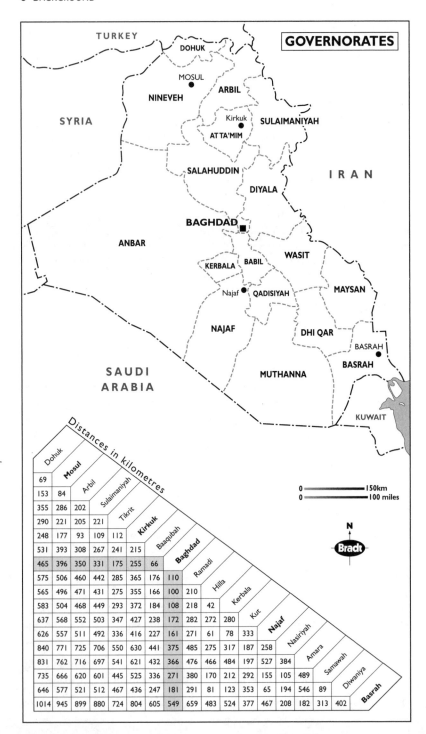

GOVERNORATES

TURKEY

DOHUK

MOSUL

NINEVEH

ARBIL

SYRIA

Kirkuk

SULAIMANIYAH

AT TA'MIM

SALAHUDDIN

IRAN

DIYALA

BAGHDAD

ANBAR

WASIT

KERBALA BABIL

Najaf QADISIYAH

MAYSAN

NAJAF

DHI QAR

BASRAH

SAUDI
ARABIA

MUTHANNA

BASRAH

KUWAIT

0 ▬▬▬▬ 150km
0 ▬▬▬▬ 100 miles

N

Bradt

Distances in kilometres																	
Dohuk																	
69	**Mosul**																
153	84	**Arbil**															
355	286	202	**Sulaimaniyah**														
290	221	205	221	**Tikrit**													
248	177	93	109	112	**Kirkuk**												
531	393	308	267	241	215	**Baaqubah**											
465	396	350	331	175	255	66	**Baghdad**										
575	506	460	442	285	365	176	110	**Ramadi**									
565	496	471	431	275	355	166	100	210	**Hilla**								
583	504	468	449	293	372	184	108	218	42	**Kerbala**							
637	568	552	503	347	427	238	172	282	272	280	**Kut**						
626	557	511	492	336	416	227	161	271	61	78	333	**Najaf**					
840	771	725	706	550	630	441	375	485	275	317	187	258	**Nasiriyah**				
831	762	716	697	541	621	432	366	476	466	484	197	527	384	**Amara**			
735	666	620	601	445	525	336	271	380	170	212	292	155	105	489	**Samawah**		
646	577	521	512	467	436	247	181	291	81	123	353	65	194	546	89	**Diwaniya**	
1014	945	899	880	724	804	605	549	659	483	524	377	467	208	182	313	402	**Basrah**

MAJOR TOWNS

Baghdad, with a population of 5,348,000, is the capital city. It lies in the heart of the Middle East, 692km southwest of Tehran (Iran) and 805km east of Beirut (Lebanon). It is an important manufacturing, trade, communications and cultural centre in the Tigris–Euphrates Valley. More than 31% of the country's population is found in Baghdad and the governorate around the capital.

Basrah and Mosul are competing for the title of Iraq's second city. Mosul lost some of its inhabitants during the 1960s and Basrah became the second-largest city during the mid 70–80s due to migration of labour to work in construction and development programmes. Since the Iran–Iraq war (1980–88) Basrah has lost a large number of its inhabitants while Mosul has gained a similar number.

Basrah (population 1,435,000), characterised by a network of canals, is often called the Venice of the East. It is Iraq's main port but, as in most coastal settlements, the pace of life tends to be leisurely and carefree. **Mosul** (population 1,000,000) is named after 'muslin', the cotton for which it is famous. The country's Christian community is concentrated in this city which is also home to Arabs, Kurds, and Turcomans.

Kirkuk (population 550,000) is Iraq's fourth-largest city. Oil was discovered in the Kirkuk area in 1927. The city is the traditional home of the country's Turcoman minority.

ECONOMY AND SANCTIONS

Oil is the mainstay of the Iraqi economy, which has been devastated since the imposition of sanctions following the invasion of Kuwait in August 1990. In 1991 oil production declined by an estimated 85% and GDP fell by two-thirds. Some damage to the infrastructure during the Gulf War is still unrepaired. Apart from the ruling clique and its supporters who benefit from the luxuries provided by a thriving black market, many Iraqis are impoverished and undernourished. The UN's Food and Agricultural Organisation's calculations show that from 1990 to 1995 food prices rose 4,000-fold, and an average wage of US$2–3 a month has forced thousands of families to sell the family silver and household items to make ends meet. Many civil servants have second and third jobs.

The main farming area is in the region of the country's two major rivers, the Tigris and Euphrates. Arable land accounts for about 12% of farmland with permanent crops 1%, meadows and pastures 9%, forest and woodland 3%. In the early 1990s, Iraq produced 1.5 million metric tons of wheat and 768,000 metric tons of barley. Rice production amounted to 189,000 tons and date production to 566,000 metric tons. Other crops include potatoes, tomatoes, cucumbers, watermelons and oranges. Livestock consists of cattle, sheep, goats and chickens. About 40% of the workforce is employed in the agricultural sector. The fishing industry is small and centred around freshwater species (see *Fauna and flora*, page 6).

The manufacturing sector is underdeveloped, the most commonly produced goods being footwear, cigarettes, construction materials, processed foods and textiles.

FEBRUARY 21 1998
Felicity Arbuthnot

I remember going to interview a woman who had lost both her husband and seven-year-old son. She had sold everything she owned to try to get medication for them and when they died she did not even have enough for the shroud cloth. I talked to her in the huge, empty living room of what had been a beautifully appointed house. As we talked, the room filled with children, creeping in, sitting on the floor, quiet as mice, watching my every move. For these incredibly hospitable, isolated people, a stranger in the neighbourhood is a rare treat. When I left, dusk was falling and as I got into the battered car the children surrounded it – about 50 of them – waving, laughing, and blowing kisses. When they could no longer keep up I looked back and the little knot in the road was still waving and blowing kisses. It was February 21 1998, the darkest night, the night we were all certain the UK and US were going to bomb again. I went back to my hotel, lay on the bed and cried and cried.

Prior to the imposition of sanctions, annual exports stood at US$10.4 billion and imports at US$6.6 billion. As well as oil, Iraq exported dates, raw wool hides and skins and imported machinery, food stuffs and pharmaceuticals. Most of the trade was conducted with the USA, the UK, Germany, France, Italy, Brazil, Turkey, and Japan. In 2001, Iraq signed free-trade agreements with six Arab states. It is looking optimistically to the future since sanctions allow it to export nothing but oil and to import only consignments agreed to by the United Nations.

Oil-for-food
Since May 1996, under UN Security Council Resolution 986, commonly referred to as the oil-for-food deal, Iraq has been allowed to export US$2 billion of oil every six months to buy food and medicine. This was increased to US$5.2 billion in 1988. UNSCR 687 calls on Iraq to destroy its chemical and biological weapons as well as its ballistic missiles. This was done under UN supervision but there were frequent confrontations with UN weapons inspectors, who were eventually expelled from the country at the end of 1998. While the regime continually claims it has complied with all UN resolutions (which it sees as a gross infringement of its sovereignty), the US, supported by Britain, is likely to veto the lifting of sanctions until Saddam Hussein is deposed, despite the opposition of Russia, France and China.

ETHNIC GROUPS AND LANGUAGES
The Iraqi people are like a necklace where the thread of nationality unites a variety of unique and colourful beads. The Arabs are in the majority, making up at least 75% of the population, while 18% are Kurds and the remaining 7%

consists of Assyrians, Turcomans and Armenians. Arabic is the official language and English is widely understood, especially in urban areas. Kurdish (Sorani dialect) is spoken in northern Iraq (generally referred to as Iraqi Kurdistan). The Turcomans converse in Turkish. Farsi is spoken by some tribal elements.

RELIGIONS

Islam is the religion of 90% of Iraqis. The Muslims are either Sunnis or Shias. The Sunnis believe that after the death of Prophet Mohammed the leadership should be in the hands of the community at large, while the Shias believe the descendants of the prophet should lead. Estimates of the number of Shias vary from 54% to 70% of Iraqis. Even though they are in a minority, the Sunnis enjoy a higher social position and favoured political status. Iraq is one of the few Arab countries where the Shia constitute a majority. Christians make up nearly 4% of the population. There is a small Jewish community and esoteric beliefs include those of the Yezidis and Mandeans.

Islam

It is important for the Western visitor to Iraq to understand how the faith of Islam affects parts of Iraq and to realise that several million of the faithful visit the country every year on pilgrimage and form the bulk of foreign visitors. Their alms and influence are very extensive even in such a state as Iraq.

Islam has five fundamental pillars: the declaration of belief that there is no God but Allah, and Mohammed is his Prophet (*shahadah*); prayers five times a day (*salat*); the giving of alms (*zakat*); fasting (*saom*); and finally, pilgrimage (*haj*) to Mecca once in a Muslim's lifetime if he has the health and financial means to do so.

Visitors to any country where Islam is the major religion should be especially sensitive to local customs during the Muslim month of Ramadan, the month in which the Koran was revealed to Prophet Mohammed. Muslims fast between the hours of sunrise and sunset during this month.

This fast can become a severe strain for participants, who cannot eat, drink, smoke or have sexual relations between sunrise and sunset, the length of

ADVICE FOR WESTERN TRAVELLERS DURING RAMADAN

- Do not smoke in the street or in public places
- Do not eat in the street
- Do not expect to find many eating places, tea houses or restaurants open during the day. In the more fundamentalist states these places will have their windows and doors blacked out or sheets screening the entrance, but they may well open discreetly for foreigners.
- Avoid provocation, which includes dressing conservatively. This is especially important for female travellers. Above all, avoid confrontation.

which varies from country to country but can be as much as 12 hours. When the temperature is over 38°C (100°F), particularly in desert lands, being without water can be a severe trial. During this month sick people and travellers are exempt, but are expected to fast for an equal number of days when they are in a position to do so.

Ramadan is observed with varying degrees of strictness in different countries. For more fundamentalist states like Iran and Saudi Arabia, Ramadan is very strict, as it is in places of pilgrimage in Iraq such as Kerbala, Najaf and Kufa. Non-Muslims will find these three towns restrictive during Ramadan.

People can become more irritable and downright ill-tempered during this month. Meals are taken late in the evening and sleeping hours can be short with early prayers. At the end of Ramadan the feast of *Eid Al Fitr* is a three- or four-day occasion where everything shuts down.

The Muslim reader will be aware of the seasons and the importance of the accompanying rituals during pilgrimages to the holy sites of Kerbala, Najaf and Kufa. After making the major pilgrimage to Mecca during the first two weeks of the Islamic month of *Dhe al-Hijja* many pilgrims follow on to Kerbala and Najaf. *Muharram* is the first month of the Islamic calander whose tenth day is *ashura,* the day of the martrydom of Hussein. Hussein, the second son of the Prophet's son-in-law Ali, refused to submit to the rule of Yazid governing from Damascus and was defeated by Yazid's soldiers at the battle of Kerbala. His martrydom is commemorated principally by the Shias and is a time of processions throughout Iran and the Shia regions of Iraq. It is a day of atonement, expressions of grief and sometimes ritual flagellation. If you want to see the processions, keep a very low profile. Accommodation will be very difficult to find in Najaf and Kerbala throughout the month of Muharram.

Lion detail, Ishtar Gate

The Ancient Kingdoms

Iraq is a jigsaw of deserts, mountains and marshes. And all around lie centuries of more-or-less remembered histories of vanished civilisations which pervade the thinking, the attitudes and the lives of the multi-racial descendants of these civilisations.

K J Whitehead, *Iraq The Irremediable* (1989)

CHRONOLOGY

3000BC	Sumer and Akkad Ancient kingdoms were the first civilisations developed on the banks of the Tigris and Euphrates.
1900BC	Babylon emerged from the union of the Sumerian and Akkadian kingdoms. Hammurabi developed his famous code of law.
1400BC	Rise of Assyria, a kingdom that conquered more than 40 nations. The Assyrians founded the largest empire of their times and built great cities such as Ashur, Nineveh and Nimrud.
606–539BC	Neo-Babylonians. One of the most famous rulers during this period was Nebuchadnezzar, who built a magnificent summer palace and the hanging gardens of Babylon.
539–330BC	Achaemanian Persians. Cyrus the Great, founder of the Achaemenid dynasty, ascended the Persian throne. He was welcomed by the Babylonians, who were the victims of a series of inefficient rulers.
331–129BC	Seleucid Greeks. Seleucus, one of Alexander the Great's generals, ruled Mesopotamia and Persia, which became known as the kingdom of the Seleucide.
130BC–AD226	Parthian Persians. A Persian tribe of nomads ruled ancient Iraq and built the city of Hatra.
AD227-636	Sassanian Persians. This dynasty challenged Roman control of eastern trade routes. During their rule many of the ancient cities of Mesopotamia were buried beneath the sand of the desert.

EARLY MESOPOTAMIA

Recorded history began at Sumer, a city state in ancient Iraq, but long before the first cities made their appearance in 3000BC Mesopotamia, the land

between the two rivers, which we now know as Iraq, was the home of pre-historic man.

Among the world's oldest human remains is a campsite, estimated to be 120,000 years old. It was found in 1949 by Dr Naji Al 'Asil, the Director General of the Iraqi Department of Antiquities. The discovery was made at Barda-Balka between the northern Iraqi cities of Kirkuk and Sulaimaniyah. Four skeletons – one 60,000 years old and the others 45,000 years old – were also discovered in northern Iraq, near the town of Rowanduz in Shanidar Cave.

The great agricultural revolution – when man stopped his wandering existence based on hunting wild beasts and gathering plants and began to domesticate animals and cultivate crops – took place in Mesopotamia around 10,000 years ago. Primitive settlements grew into towns and villages, which eventually evolved into city states along the banks of the Tigris and Euphrates. Writing was developed to record commercial transactions; ceremonies and rituals became part of everyday life. Even the British coronation ceremony has traces of Mesopotamian practices, as do present-day baptismal rituals.

As Samuel Noah Kramer points out in the book *Cradle of Civilisation*:

> The Mesopotamians were the first people on earth to live in cities,
> study the stars, use the arch and wheeled vehicles, write epic poetry and
> compile a legal code. They also manufactured linen, built sailing ships,
> laid the foundations of astrology and for 3,000 years engaged in serious

scholarship which left its mark on the science, mathematics, medicine, literature, philosophy and religion of subsequent civilisations.

The concept of the tablet of destinies is found in Mesopotamian mythology and in the Jewish tradition where Moses receives the Torah on two tablets. In the Koran, the Book of Faith mentioned in verse 85 is said to come from heavenly tablets, which were subsequently referred to by Henry IV in Shakespeare's drama: 'O God! That one might read the Book of Fate and see the revolution of the times'. In Uruk (3800–3200BC) cuneiform manuals explained the meaning of dreams. Dream books continued to be used in Byzantine times and in the 20th century had a bearing on Freud's Interpretation of Dreams.

Leonard Woolley, who conducted extensive excavations at Ur's royal cemetery during the 1930s, draws attention to the legacy of ancient Iraq when he asks:

> How many of us realise that our superstitious impulse to turn back
> when a black cat crosses our path stems from the people of Babylon?
> Do they come to mind when we look at the twelve divisions on our
> watch-face, when we buy eggs by the shock (sixty), when we look up
> at the stars to read our fate in their movement and conjunctions?

The Mesopotamian influence spread through conquest, trade, and travelling scholars. The Babylonian cloak was worn from India to Italy, and Mesopotamian goods such as belts and sandals were found in Roman markets. The Bible tells how in the 2nd millennium bc the King of Moab summoned a scholar from Pitru on the Euphrates because of his knowledge of cuneiform texts.

In *The Legacy of Mesopotamia*, which she edited, Stephanie Dalley describes how the Babylonians took foreigners captive in battle and brought them back to Mesopotamia.

> Eventually those people might return home, whether for retirement
> or because they were ransomed, taking with them reports of the
> marvels they had seen and learnt abroad. Some wonders were
> practical, such as the pilastered façades of temples, brick vaulting, and
> other technical skills; others were intellectual, such as the principles
> on which harps were turned, or the basis of astronomy.

In the final chapter of the book, Henrietta McCall concludes:

> No one concerned with the origins of Western civilisation can afford
> to disregard its roots in Mesopotamia and the legends handed down
> to us. It does not matter that there is so little above ground: no
> pyramid, no temple, no hypostyle hall, theatre or circus, no forum, no
> colonnade, only the remains of a few crumbling ziggurats. The visible
> splendour of proud Babylon and mighty Nineveh may have
> disappeared from sight but the dusty mounds that remain are linked
> with the very start of recorded history. Thus their legacy is
> unassailable, their renown indelible: legendary, glorious, immortal.

BEFORE SUMER

Ancient Iraq's early farming communities made their appearance between 9000 and 5000BC. Women, anxious to have a fixed abode in which to raise their children, influenced the decision to abandon the nomadic hunter-gatherer life-style, as did a decline in edible plants and animals. Jarmo, founded in 6500BC in the foothills of the Zagros Mountains, is one of the oldest known permanent settlements whose inhabitants lived in mud houses, weaved flax and used tools such as sickles made of obsidian. They buried their dead underneath the floors of their dwellings, a practice that continued in Sumerian times.

People from the Hassuna culture, which dates back to 6000BC, introduced irrigation, were accomplished potters and embarked on trade from the Persian Gulf to the Mediterranean. Some of the world's finest ceramics were produced during the Halaf period (5000BC) which followed. The villages now had cobbled streets and animals grazed in the surrounding fields. Copper beads replaced clay and stone jewellery.

During the Ubaid period (5000BC) the settlements along the Tigris and Euphrates, including Eridu, Ur, Lagash, Nippur and Kish (the forerunners of the Sumerian city states) were built around a shrine. The primitive irrigation system was augmented with small canals and reservoirs, and historians have commented on the division of labour that became evident in society.

The Uruk period (3800–3200BC) was a time of rapid urbanisation. As many as 45,000 people lived in the city of Uruk itself. A collection of temples were dedicated to the goddess Inanna, queen of heaven and earth, and decorated with mosaics and frescoes.The temples became a hive of commercial activity where craftsmen plied their trade. The first pictographics (pictures of objects) were developed here as trade could not be conducted without written records, and so writing began. Cylinder seals used for signatures were also an invention of the people of Uruk. The story of the seven sages, part of Mesopotamian mythology dating back to 3000BC, tells of how one of the great gods despatched seven wise men to the cities to spread knowledge that ranged from music and metallurgy to agriculture and construction.

The Jemdat Nasr period (3200–2900BC) built on the achievements of Uruk. The story of the flood, another Mesopotamian myth which has striking parallels to the biblical story of Noah, is believed to date back to this period. Floods were a common occurrence in Mesopotamian life, but it seems that there was one great flood, which is written about in the *Epic of Gilgamesh*. In this epic Ut-Napishtim, the good, wise man, received a warning from the Gods:

> Tear down this house, build a ship!
> Aboard the ship take thou the seed of all living things.
> The ship that thou shalt build
> Her dimensions shall be to measure
> Equal shall be her width and her length

The importance of the flood is evident from the break in the list of Sumerian kings compiled by the kings' spin doctors (who recorded the exploits of their masters). These chroniclers noted: 'Then came the flood and after the flood kingship again descended from heaven.'

THE SUMERIANS

The seeds of Sumerian culture sown in Iraq's pre-history germinated during the Hassuna, Halaf, Ubaid, Uruk and Jemdat Nasr periods and blossomed in the city-states of the third millennium BC, among them Sippar, Kish, Akshak, Larak, Nippur, Adab, Umma, Lagash, Bad-tibira, Uruk, Larsa, Ur and Eridu.

Introduction

The cities began as simple agricultural settlements on the fertile banks of the Tigris and Euphrates. Regular supplies of fish and birds could be relied on if there was a problem with crops. Floods, however, were unpredictable, building materials had to be imported, and the inhabitants of Mesopotamia fought three main battles: the battle against nature, the battle against other cities who wanted to expand their boundaries, and the battle against foreign invaders. After their phenomenal expansion the empires were plagued by internal disputes and were frequently dealt a death blow by their neighbours. Some conquerors assimilated the culture and wisdom of the vanquished while others were only interested in pillage and destruction.

Worship

There was no rational explanation for the forces of nature in the Mesopotamian view of the world, which was run by gods who had to be obeyed and honoured. Fear of the gods, whose decisions could not be understood, resulted in the emergence of an elaborate system of worship centred on the temples whose requirements controlled the lives of the cities' inhabitants. By 2500BC much of the land in Sumer was temple-owned and the farmers laboured in the service of the gods. The Sumerians developed a meticulous system of record keeping. The bureaucratic civil service left them in no doubt about what was due to them and what they owed to the temple. Merchants and craftsmen also worked for the temples, the major employer of the time.

The gods, who were treated like human beings, had to receive regular meals and ablutions and were honoured with elaborate rites and rituals. The image of the god was placed in a small room to which only the priests had access. Sometimes they slept next to the statue in the hope that the god would speak to them in a dream.

The hierarchical nature of Mesopotamian society, composed of the aristocracy, the citizens and the slaves, was reflected in the concept of the world of the gods populated by numerous deities of varying status. The common people prayed to their household gods or to the gods who were only honoured with a small chapel in the street. The peasant normally dealt with Ashnan the barley god or Shumuqan the cattle god. But in times of crisis the gods at the top of the spiritual hierarchy – such as the moon god Nanna (who knew the future), Ninurta the warrior-god, the mother earth goddess

Ninhursag, and Ishtar the goddess of love and procreation – could be contacted through the intercession of the priests or with the assistance of the personal god, a special diety to which the individual prayed. The king had to answer to the supreme deity, hence the magnificent temples built in the service of the gods to secure their favour and protection. Ur, possibly the home of Abraham, was constructed around the mud-brick ziggurat dedicated to the moon god and his wife. The construction of temples and ziggurats was a major preoccupation of the Mesopotamians. Beer was brewed in the temples to make life more pleasant for the workers who laboured on the magnificent structures and brewing even had a patron goddess, Ishtar. Since excavations of the ancient cities began in the 19th century more than 30 ziggurats have been unearthed. Georges Roux, author of *Ancient Iraq*, likens them to 'prayers of bricks – they extended to the gods a permanent invitation to descend on earth at the same time as they expressed one of man's most remarkable efforts to rise above his miserable condition and to establish closer contacts with divinity'.

But sacrifices and fine buildings to house the deities were not enough; there was also an emphasis on good deeds and actions which has a striking resemblance to the dictates of the Bible. Georges Roux says that the favours of the gods went to those who led a good life, who were good parents, good sons, good neighbours, good citizens and who practised virtues as highly esteemed then as they are now: kindness and compassion, righteousness and sincerity, justice, respect of the law and of the established order. Every day worship your god, says a Babylonian 'Council of Wisdom', but also:

> To the feeble show kindness
> Do not insult the downtrodden
> Do charitable deeds, render service all your days
> Do not utter libel, speak what is of good report
> Do not say evil things, speak well of people

The written word

In addition to their religious functions, temples were the focal point of community life and the source of inventions that changed the world, such as the development of writing. Pictographic tablets, said to have made their first appearance in Eanna's temple in Uruk (see page 148) came into everyday use. The primary motivation was the recording of commercial transactions. If pots were to be exchanged, pictures, which dried in the sun, were drawn in wet mud. The pictures subsequently became impressionistic lines, and the term 'cuneiform', which means wedge-shaped, was coined to describe this form of writing. As the number of characters became unmanageable, phonetic writing developed: symbols (letters) denoting the pronunciation of the word evolved. A new class of scribes were plying their trade by 3000BC and, in addition to commercial transactions, the Sumerians recorded their history and their myths, including the *Epic of Gilgamesh*, the world's oldest literary work (see page 22). A list of kings was also compiled. Before the Seleucid era in 311BC there was no calendar and years were referred to according to the rulers, for example the 12th year of Nabuy-na'id, King of Babylon. Around 30,000 inscribed tablets have been unearthed from Sumerian and Akkadian times, some from great libraries in the cities.

Mastering the art of writing was a serious undertaking. Scribes went to special schools, attached to the temples, where the hours were long, the discipline rigorous and the teaching concentrated largely on rote learning and memorisation of word lists. The first dictionaries were compiled and scholars were eager to pursue their own lines of inquiry and contribute to disciplines such as science and mathematics. Mesopotamian schools could therefore be described as the forerunners of universities.

Royal palaces

The second power-house of Mesopotamian city-states was the royal palace. A symbiotic relationship developed between the kings and the priests: the temples made certain that taxes were paid to the palace and the kings built fine temples and showed due reverence to the gods whose protection and favour were continually invoked.

While never neglecting their religious duties the kings also devoted great care and attention to their palaces, which were stocked with the finest imports from far-off lands and displayed with pride. A palace in the city of Mari in western Mesopotamia, which was destroyed by Hammurabi in the 18th century BC, had 300 rooms and covered seven acres.

But the kings did not just sit in their ivory towers. They held public audiences and took an interest in the affairs of the cities. They were the arbiters in important law suites, despatched troops to subdue troublesome nomadic tribes who were making incursions into farmland and discussed commercial alliances with envoys from other courts. The palaces were also places of entertainment, where female slaves, who received musical tuition, played the harp and poets were among the regular performers.

Like the temples, the palaces were economic institutions in their own right, which sponsored thriving industries and efficient agricultural production. Workers were paid in food and clothing and were eager to avoid the 'private sector' where they were more likely to fall into a vicious cycle of debt from which it was difficult to emerge.

Social structure

Apart from the palaces and temples, a number of rich and powerful families owned land. From this aristocratic group the king drew his advisors and the temple its senior priests. The farmers ensured a regular food supply and the rest of the population was free to pursue specialised occupations: carpentry, tanning, baking, brewing, pottery, brick and cloth making. The arts, especially sculpture and painting, developed and glass was made as early as 2500BC.

The workers toiled away in small, sprawling streets. There was no such thing as town planning, a sewage system or garbage disposal in the cities, which had expanded from small villages along the river banks to house up to 100,000 inhabitants. The lower class had to be content with one-storey mud-brick houses. The better-off had a two-storey house with a reception room for guests, kitchen, bathroom and sometimes servants' quarters, a workshop and storeroom on the ground floor, and the family rooms upstairs. During the hot summer months family members often slept on the roof. Household gods were worshipped in a small chapel and deceased family members were buried in a small mausoleum.

Public squares were places of entertainment where professional story-tellers told their tales. Amusements included games of chance, wrestling and chariot racing. The bazaars with stalls overflowing with local and imported items, taverns and restaurants serving grilled fish and meat bore a striking resemblance to bazaars throughout the Middle East today. In Sumer the bricklayers, like their present-day counterparts, worked with standard bricks, drank beer and lived in cities administered by civil servants. The mud houses in the villages of present-day Iraq do not differ much from their Sumerian counterparts: hence the comment from Georges Roux, author of *Ancient Iraq*, that there are few countries in the world where the past is more strangely alive, where the historian's dead texts are provided with a more appropriate illustration.

The merchants traded grain, wool and textiles for essential building materials such as timber and an extensive trade network with the Near East developed. The main imports included gold, silver, copper and lead, and luxury items such as ivory, pearls and shells. Caravans journeyed to the Mediterranean coast and Iran while boats reached Somaliland and Ethiopia. Information about other cultures was an important commodity and merchants were a vital link in exchanges with foreigners.

It is a tribute to the humanity of ancient Iraq that the lowest class, the slaves, had rights, could take part in business, borrow money and purchase their freedom. Freemen could sell themselves and their families into slavery to pay off debts. Reforms were introduced against exploitation by the priestly class, who charged exorbitantly for burials and other services.

Early settlements

The walled cities produced security and stability. Primary allegiance shifted from the family to the group and unity was fostered by faith in personal gods who protected every settlement and city. The civil service and political institutions could function and develop and there was time to engage in cultural and leisurely pursuits. The Mesopotamians had a passion for organisation and routine, and this characterised all their settlements.

But the growth of cities with fixed boundaries resulted in boundary disputes, a recurrent theme in the history of the Middle East. Each city relied on a section of irrigated land for its survival and the history of Mesopotamia was largely the history of wars and disputes between various city-states, each eager to assert its authority over the whole region.

The early settlements were fledgling democracies governed by assemblies appointed by the citizens. But in the face of military threats the citizens felt they needed a leader to ensure their victory in boundary disputes. The term 'big man' (*lugal*) was used to refer to the first leaders who were only appointed for the duration of a particular conflict. But as the conflicts became more frequent, the leaders became permanent and the institution of kingship developed.

Early history

Gilgamesh was one of the legendary early kings of the city of Uruk around 2600BC, whose fame was assured by the building of the city walls. He emerged victorious in intercity disputes but his major preoccupation in life was the quest for immortality, the theme of one of man's earliest epics. The prototype of Heracles and Ulysses, the *Epic of Gilgamesh*, is the tale of the exploits of Gilgamesh. It spread throughout the ancient Near East. The exploits of certain other ancient rulers left such an impression on their subjects that they were deified. Dumuzi, for example, became the fertility god.

A frequently documented dispute between the city-states occurred in 2700BC when the people of Umma removed the stele (boundary marker) of their city and marched into the plain of Lagash. In ancient times boundary disputes assumed a religious-metaphysical character as both cities resorted to the assistance of their 'guardian gods'.

The priests, meanwhile, were starting to exploit their status and power, prompting Urukagina, the peace-loving, idealistic reformer King of Lagash, to introduce a number of anti-corruption measures so that the high priest was not able to 'come into the garden of a poor mother and take wood therefrom nor fruit in tax therefrom'. The Mesopotamians also pioneered the concept of freedom of the individual.

The city-states were united in the 24th century BC by Sargon, King of Akkad, an area northwest of the Sumerian kingdoms where modern Baghdad now stands and inhabited by Semitic people. Akkadian was adopted as the language of diplomacy and Sargon's empire sprawled into Persia, Syria and along the Mediterranean coast into Lebanon. Sargon proved that a man of humble origins could rise to the highest office. The story of his birth, retold by Leonard Cottrell in *Land of the Two Rivers*, bears a striking resemblance to that of Moses:

> Sargon the mighty, King of Akkad am I
> My mother was lowly, my father I knew not,
> The brother of my father dwelt in the mountains.
> My city is Azupiranu, which lieth on the bank of the Euphrates.
> My lowly mother conceived me, in secret she brought me forth.
> She cast me into the river, which [rose] over me.
> The river bore me up, unto Akki, the irrigator, it carried me,
> Akki the irrigator reared me up,
> Akki the irrigator as his gardener appointed me.
> When I was his gardener the goddess Ishtar loved me,
> And of fifty-four years I ruled the kingdom.

Sargon does not provide a detailed account of how he rose from the position of a cupbearer to the King of Kish to establish the first empire in history.

THE EPIC OF GILGAMESH

The story begins in the city of Uruk where Gilgamesh has his designs on 'the warrior's daughter and the nobleman's spouse'. The citizens ask the gods to intervene and Anu obliges by creating Enkidu, a wild character who lives with the beasts and upsets hunters. Gilgamesh decides to ensnare him and enlists the services of a prostitute who is given the job of seducing and civilising Enkidu. She succeeds and Enkidu confronts Gilgamesh when he comes to avail himself of the services of the seductress. They start to fight, but a mutual affection defuses the hostility and the two friends set out to confront the giant of the forest, Humbaba. The god Shamash comes to their rescue by sending the winds against Humbaba, whose head is cut off.

The next confrontation is with the goddess Ishtar who falls in love with Gilgamesh but he spurns her advances and reminds her of the way in which her previous lovers were treated: one was turned into a wolf, another into a spider.

Ishtar responds by sending the bull of heaven to destroy the city of Uruk. With Enkidu's help Gilgamesh slays the bull and throws its right thigh at Ishtar. Such an insult cannot go unpunished and the gods decide Enkidu should die. After losing his friend, Gilgamesh searches for eternal life. He travels to meet Ut-napishtim, whom the gods made immortal after he survived the great flood. Ut-napishtim has some sobering words for Gilgamesh:

> Do we build houses for ever?
> Does the river for ever raise up and bring on floods?
> The dragon-fly leaves it shell
> That its face might but glance at the face of the sun.
> Since the days of yore there has been no permanence;
> The resting and the dead, how alike they are!

Ut-napishtim instructs Gilgamesh to find the plant of life. Gilgamesh dives into the depths of the ocean and picks the plant, which is eaten by a snake when he falls asleep. He then returns to Uruk and embarks on a building programme to ensure his memory lives on.

The message of the epic is that any individual is mortal but the city, meaning the community as well as the buildings, lives on.

During his reign he built the mighty ziggurat at Nippur and brought exotic plants to his kingdom in the hope that they would acclimatise and flourish.

After the death of Sargon's son, eastern barbarians known as the Guti destroyed the empire and wiped Agade, Sargon's capital, off the map. Utuhegal, the ruler of Uruk, drove out the invaders only to be deposed by one of his generals, Ur Nammu, who founded the third dynasty of Ur (2113–2006BC). The kingdoms of Sumer and Ur were united once more. But the unity was more of a partnership in which Ur, with its temple to the moon goddess and 80ft ziggurat, was the senior partner. Despite his usurpation of power, Ur Nammu presided over the Sumerian renaissance, a time of increased prosperity during which the arts were given a new lease of life. Ur Nammu continued the tradition of concern for fairness and justice and inscribed the first law code on cuneiform tablets, three centuries before Hammurabi's renowned 8ft stele of black diorite with 282 laws. The Sumerian renaissance continued under Ur Nammu's son, Shulgi.

Ur fell after an attack by the Amorites, Semitic nomads from the deserts of Syria and Arabia, and Elamites from an ancient kingdom east of the Tigris. The attack was a watershed in the history of ancient Iraq: city-states were replaced by small kingdoms and kings rented out land. A society in which the temples were the focus of economic activity was replaced by a society of farmers, citizens and traders.

In the book *Cradle of Civilisation*, Samuel Noah Kramer describes how the calamity that had overtaken their land and cities made a deep impression on the poets of Sumer's final days. One of their lamentations may serve as a melancholy epitaph for the people who, more than ten centuries earlier, first crossed the threshold of civilisation and whose brilliant achievements have enriched most of the great cultures since. It bemoans the day

> That law and order cease to exist...
> That cities be destroyed, that houses be destroyed...
> That [Sumer's] rivers flow with bitter water...
> That the mother care not for her children...
> That kingship be carried off from the land...
> That on the banks of the Tigris and Euphrates...
> there grow stickily plants

BABYLON AND HAMMURABI

After the Amorite conquest warfare plagued the region as power shifted between rival princes, but in 1780BC Hammurabi, 6th King of Babylon, once again united Mesopotamia. For him unity meant a centralised administration backed up by the rule of law and an efficient system of justice implemented by magistrates under his control.

Hammurabi was a man of patience and foresight. Before embarking on his empire-building he spent 25 years cementing military and political alliances. His empire, with Babylon as its capital, extended northward from the Persian Gulf through the Tigris and Euphrates river valleys and westward to the coast of the Mediterranean sea. Roads were improved to facilitate trade and to enable troops to move quickly and execute their orders. Fifty-five of Hammurabi's official letters to local governors have been discovered. Even ordinary citizens wrote to their ruler. Messengers ensured the efficient flow of correspondence. Even after Babylon's political significance was eclipsed it was respected as an enlightened cultural centre. It was here that the stories of Gilgamesh were brought together in one long epic.

Legal precedent

Despite his impressive record as an empire builder, however, Hammurabi is remembered mainly for his famous code of law, which deals with personal property, real estate, trade and business, the family, injuries, labour and rates of pay. A sense of fairness and social justice seems to be the guiding principle and no one is excluded from legal protection. Workers are assured of a living wage but skill is rewarded with higher remuneration. There is no discrimination against women in business dealings: along with their male counterparts they can buy and sell properties and initiate legal proceedings.

Crimes and punishments are set out in detail: 'If the wife of a man has been caught while lying with another man, they shall bind them and throw them into the water. The husband may spare his wife and the king in turn may spare his subject.' Some of the most severe punishments are prescribed for negligent workmanship: 'If a builder constructed a house for a man but did not make his work strong, with the result that the house which he built collapsed and so has caused the death of the owner of the house, that builder shall be put to death.' At the end of the code divine retribution is invoked on whoever alters the just laws. The Babylonians were litigation happy and eager to bring lawsuits especially in property transactions.

The 282 laws outlined in 3000 lines of cuneiform can today be seen in the Louvre Museum in Paris. In the 12th century BC the Elamites sequestrated the stele on which the laws are inscribed as war booty and took it to Susa. It was discovered by the French in 1901.

Evolution of religion

The social transformation of Babylon, in which the rule of law played a central part, was accompanied by a change in the hierarchy of the gods. Marduk, the warrior god, was elevated to the status of supreme being in place of Enlil, the head of the Sumerian pantheon.

But despite the magnificence of their empire the Babylonians remained pessimistic. They never forgot that the life-giving rivers could also bring devastation and the forces of nature could wipe out their newly found order.

The *Epic of Creation*, a Mesopotamian myth, describes how order was created from a watery chaos when Abzu the sweet waters and Timat the sea created the universe and the gods. Abzu was destroyed by Enki, the god of wisdom, when he conspired against the gods, but Timat continued the conflict and no one could stop her. Enki's son Marduk made a deal with the gods. He would subdue Timat if he was made head of the gods. They agreed. After Timat was slain Marduk used half of her body to make the sky. Man was made out of the blood of a god who fought alongside Timat.

The Babylonians believed that chaos could return at the beginning of the new year. The struggle in the cosmos, described in the *Epic of Creation*, was not brought to an end. The gods had established order but they could still be challenged by the forces of chaos, and an elaborate New Year festival was held to elicit the favour of the gods and ensure order prevailed for another year.

After Hammurabi's death in 1750BC his empire was ravaged by the Hittites, a mountain people from Anatolia, who spared Babylon. The next rulers were the Kassites, a mountain people from Persia, who assimilated Babylonian traditions. They signed a frontier agreement with the Assyrian princes and their rule was characterised by peace and stability until they were overthrown by the Elamites in 1168BC.

THE ASSYRIANS

The Assyrians, Mesopotamia's next rulers, perfected the art of war and conquest and succeeded in establishing their grip on nearly all of the Near East. They came from the state of Assyria in the north, centred around four cities: Ashur, Arbil, Nimrud and Nineveh. At the height of their power Egypt was nothing more than an Assyrian province. The Assyrian empire stretched for a thousand miles from the Nile Valley in Egypt to the Caucasus Mountains in Armenia.

The conquests had a religious dimension: the enemies of the king were also the enemies of the god Ashur. Just as Ashur stood at the head of the religious hierarchy, his man on earth, the King of Assyria, had to stand at the head of all other rulers, and battles were seen as crusades.

Conquests went hand in hand with the brutal slaying of the inhabitants of cities that had been subdued. Victory was the Assyrians' *raison d'etre*, war was a way of life and the spreading of terror was their speciality. Shalmaneser III (858–824BC) reigned for 35 years; 31 years were spent fighting. The vanquished had to pay tribute, a form of protection money, to ensure their settlements were left standing. Military exploits were immortalised in magnificent works of art. The Assyrians are remembered mainly for their reliefs (designs standing out from the surface into which they have been carved): winged bull-men and lion-men who look down from the gates of palaces. The walls of palaces were decorated with war scenes sculptured on limestone. The sculptures also had a propaganda message: remain subservient to the conquerors or perish. Art was no longer a medium for glorifying the gods: it now depicted the exploits of kings and armies.

The army made the Assyrians mighty. As Georges Roux points out in *Ancient Iraq*, the army's success lay 'in the quality of its troops, the superiority of its weapons and the rigidity of its discipline. Originally a conscript army was recruited among the peasants of northern Iraq, a mixed race of born warriors who combined the boldness of the bedouin with the tenacity of the farmer and the toughness of the highlander'. Tigalathpileser III set up a permanent army, which consisted of troops from throughout the empire: the horsemen were from Iran, the camel-drivers from Arabia. The use of horse-drawn chariots was fully exploited and ingenious siege weapons for demolishing city walls were developed. The Assyrians never referred to their casualties and the figures for their soldiers were probably inflated; at the battle of Qarqar, Shalmaneser III claims to have commanded 120,000 men.

MESOPOTAMIAN MYTHS

The *Epic of Creation* is described in detail by Leonard Cottrell in *Land of the Two Rivers:*

'Every year at the winter solstice the Babylonians gathered to devote eleven days to ensuring the gods' proper attention to their duties during the coming year.

'First for several days they purified themselves by fasting, ceremonial washing and the like. On the fifth day the priests escorted the king to the shrine of the god Marduk; then followed a dramatic incident, which reminds us that all play-acting originated in religious ritual. The king was left alone for a time in the god's shrine. Then the high priest emerged from his sanctuary. He approached the king, took from the monarch his royal robes and crown, forced him to his knees, and then slapped his face and pulled his ears!

'On his knees before the god's image the king had now to recite the so-called negative confessions:

> We have not sinned, O Lord of the lands,
> I have not been negligent regarding thy divinity,
> I have not destroyed Babylon.

'Then having made his confession, the king was given absolution and a blessing, after which he could put on his regalia again.

'Meanwhile in the teeming streets of the city, far below the ziggurat in which this drama was enacted, the citizens were acting out their own play. In this they were supposed to be searching for Marduk, who, according to their beliefs, had been held captive in the underworld. Unless he was brought back, the land could not prosper so mock battles took place between his supporters and those supposed to be detaining him. On the sixth or seventh day he was released by his son and avenger Nebo. On the eighth day the statue of the restored god Marduk was placed in the Chamber of Destinies together with those of all the other gods who thus presented him with their combined strength in the coming battle against the forces of Chaos. This was in order to determine "the destinies", that is the fate of society for the coming year. Later, this earthly king, grasping the hand of Marduk's image, was carried along the Sacred Way to the Festival House. Probably another mock battle took place, and then, on the eleventh day, high in the ziggurat, the sacred marriage was celebrated between Marduk and the goddess Ishtar; the deities were represented by the king and a priestess – who may have been of the royal blood.

'Finally on the twelfth day all the gods were reassembled in the Chamber of Destinies to ratify their decrees. And so the new year could begin.'

Administration

The exploits on the battlefield were not matched by an enlightened administration of conquered territories despite the development of a bureaucracy. This oversight was largely responsible for the collapse of the empire. Rule by terror did not inspire loyalty, the vanquished revolted and their revolts were brutally suppressed. Thousands of troublesome subjects were deported to other areas of the vast empire. Areas which came under Assyrian hegemony were regarded as provinces. The conquerors were interested in collecting taxes; they took much, gave little and were despised as cruel masters. The loyalty of governors was sought through a combination of rewards and threats; the threat of punishment if they deviated from the oath of obedience, and rewards in the form of a share in the royal estates and the spoils of war.

As well as having to be on their guard against uprisings in the 'provinces', the Assyrian kings had to curb dissent among their own ruling class. There were disagreements among the nobles regarding the king's successor who was supposed to have been chosen in consultation with the gods, including the sun god Ashur.

Assyrian kings ruled much like their predecessors: they ensured temples were built and maintained, they received reports from the governors of outlying provinces and built magnificent palaces. Society was made up of aristocrats who included the king's advisers, often magnificently wealthy individuals with their own courts, and free professional men, including traders, merchants, bankers, physicians and scribes. The craftsmen were organised into guilds, and fathers handed their skills down to sons. The lower class consisted of agricultural labourers, ordinary soldiers and slaves. Prisoners of war were at the bottom of the social hierarchy.

Culture and learning

The Assyrians also had an artistic side to their bloodthirsty nature and valued scholarship and science. The literary and scientific works of the Sumerians, Akkadians and Babylonians were collected in a magnificent library by Ashurbanipal, who issued an instruction in one of his letters:

> Hunt for the valuable tablets which are in your archives and which do
> not exist in Assyria and send them to me. I have written to the
> officials and overseers and no one shall withhold a tablet from you.

Temple libraries were found in all of Assyria's major towns. Ivory work was a speciality of the Assyrians. They used it to decorate thrones and it was incorporated into boxes, vases and handles or inlaid with semi-precious stones. An impressive array of bronze, gold and silver plates, cups and ornaments has been unearthed. Female slaves wove carpets and they were also experts in metal work. The Assyrians made a contribution to mathematics, astrology and medicine but restricted their studies to the collection of data. Metaphysical doctrines, such as those that attributed sickness to a punishment from the gods for past misdemeanours, hindered the development of scientific

MESOPOTAMIAN REVIVAL

The aesthetic side of Assyrian culture was greatly admired in Victorian England and once some of the reliefs had made their way to the British Museum a great interest in the history of ancient Iraq was generated. As Henrietta McCall points out in the final chapter of *The Legacy of Mesopotamia*, edited by Stephanie Dalley, it took the form of paintings (John Martin painted the *Fall of Babylon* in 1819, *The Fall of Nineveh* in 1828 and *Belshazzar's Feast* in 1820); drama (Charles Kean's theatrical production of *Sardanapalus King of Assyria* was performed in 1853); cinema (the film *Intolerance* was devoted to the fall of Babylon); and fashion. (In 1917 *Photoplay* magazine featured sketches of Babylonian dresses that were copied, Assyrian-style jewellery was on display at the Great Exhibition in 1851 and the Assyrian-style buildings designed by Alexander Thomson are still standing in Glasgow's Argyle Street.) The Revd Archibald H Sayce even published an Assyrian grammar book.

theories. Important decisions were seldom taken without consulting diviners who interpreted omens: when a star shines forth like a torch from the sunrise and in the sunset fades away, the army of the enemy will attack in force.

The Assyrian Empire

The Assyrians started to make their presence felt when Babylon was ruled by the Kassites (see page 25) and insisted that Assyria was regarded as an equal by the Kassite dynasty. The first phase of spectacular conquests began in the 11th century BC when Tiglath-Pileser I's armies reached the Mediterranean and the Assyrians began to receive tributes from Phoenician cities such as Byblos and Sidon. The gods had to be honoured, the main temple of Ashur in the capital Nineveh was restored and the waters of a tributary of the Tigris were diverted to water the capital's parks.

The brutal hallmarks of Assyrian conquest are summarised in Tiglath-Pileser's account of how he dealt with the Anatolians who were endangering the region north of Nineveh:

> With their twenty thousand warriors and their five kings I fought and defeated them. Their blood I let flow in the valleys and on the high levels of the mountains. I cut off their heads and outside their cities like heaps of grain, I piled them up. I burned their cities, with fire, I demolished them, I cleared them away.

But despite his successes on the battlefield he failed to establish an efficient administration, the conquered people revolted in 1080BC and the mighty empire was reduced to a small strip of land on the Tigris stretching for no more than 100 miles.

The Assyrian Empire rose again 150 years later. One of its rulers, Assurnasirpal II had many claims to fame including the slaying of 1,000 lions.

THE EAGLE PATROL

Tales from the past recounted by Assyrian communities, which have not been verified by historians, describe eagle-assisted flight prompted by the Assyrians' desire for conquest. Before the eagles were put in flight they were kept indoors blindfolded and without food. They were then attached to strong woven baskets that could accommodate a boy. The basket was fastened to the body of the eagles, similar to a horse and carriage (see diagram). The 'pilot' would carry a long cane to which fresh meat was attached with a hook. The starving eagles would take off and fly to get the bait, lifting the basket and the boy into the air so he could fly above enemy territory observing the strength, defence positions and military installations of the enemy.

The Assyrians once again established their domination over Phoenician cities and returned home with precious stones and metals, wood and exotic animals. Like most Assyrian rulers Assurnasirpal delighted in both barbarity and beauty. He was fond of describing how he covered a pillar with the skins of his captives. He also built a six-acre palace at Nimrud:

> A palace of cedar, cypress, juniper, boxwood, mulberry, pistachio-
> wood and tamarisk for my royal dwelling and for my lordly pleasure
> for all time I founded therein. Beasts of the mountains and the seas of
> white limestone and alabaster I fashioned and set them in the gates.

George Roux describes a magnificent ten-day feast attended by 69,574 guests in Assurnasirpal's new palace.

The conquests continued under Tiglath-Pileser III (745–727BC) and the army grew through the recruitment of foreign mercenaries. War chariots were replaced with cavalry. He tried to reform the administration and curb the disproportionate power of the nobles. The practice of mass deportations began: in total an estimated four and a half million people were deported from their traditional homes and resettled in other parts of the empire. Among them were 30,000 Syrians from Hama who were sent to the Zagros mountains, while 18,000 Arameans from the Tigris area were sent to northern Syria.

The fall of Babylon

Sargon had to devote much of his time to quashing revolts. The capital was moved to Sharrukin (present-day Khorsabad) and protected with mud-brick walls more than 75ft thick. Sargon's son, Sennacherib, turned Nineveh into a magnificent capital where 50 miles of paved canal transported water from the Gomel River – the Tigris was not clean enough! These hydraulic works boosted agriculture. But Sennacherib will be remembered mainly for his savage revenge on Babylon, spared by previous conquerors due to its cultural legacy. The Babylonians formed an anti-Assyrian alliance with the Elamites and had to be taught a lesson:

> With [the corpses of its inhabitants] I filled the city squares. The city
> and houses from its foundations to its top, I destroyed, I devastated, I
> burned with fire.

The Old Testament's Second Book of Kings describes how his forces captured 46 cities in Palestine and besieged Jerusalem where dissent was also brewing. Sennacherib was killed by a death-blow from a statue of a god: the heavenly beings could not leave the destruction of Babylon unavenged.

Esarhaddon, one of Sennacherib's sons, was a humanitarian ruler who offered food to the famine-stricken people of Elam. He also rebuilt Babylon in 671BC. But the Assyrians were not learning the lessons of history: they never understood how to deal fairly with their subjects and they continued fighting among themselves.

Despite his military and scholarly achievements, Ashurbanipal (668–627BC) laments:

> I cannot do away with the strife in my country and the dissensions in
> my family; disturbing scandals oppress me always. Illness of mind and
> flesh bow me down; with cries of woe I bring my days to an end. On
> the day of the city god, the day of the festival I am wretched; death is
> seizing hold upon me and bears me down.

The end of the empire

The Assyrian Empire was dealt a swift death-blow in 612BC when the Babylonian King Nabopolassar joined forces with the Elamites and the Medes, a young and little-known people of the Iranian Plateau from whom the Kurds are said to be descendent, and led a combined attack against Nineveh.

The disintegration of the Sumerian city-states was lamented, the downfall of Babylon was mourned, but no one shed a tear at the collapse of the hated Assyrian giant.

BABYLON REVISITED

The Neo-Babylonians ended Assyrian supremacy and resurrected Babylon to its former glory through a dazzling renaissance of Mesopotamia presided over by Nebuchadnezzar II, who was crowned on the death of King Nabopolassar in 605BC.

It was essentially a religious revival accompanied by an extensive building programme, which focused on the restoration of religious shrines to long-revered Babylonian gods, with an emphasis on religious rituals, especially the New Year festival. The most magnificent was Marduk's temple. Nebuchadnezzar proudly tells us:

> Silver, gold, costly precious stones, bronze, wood from Magan, everything that is expensive, glittering abundance, the products of the mountains, the treasures of the seas, large quantities (of goods) sumptuous gifts, I brought to my city of Babylon before him (Marduk).

Babylon was also the home of the Tower of Babel, a 300ft ziggurat and 1,179 temples, which once again became the focal point of economic activity. They had their employees as well as a class of people who laboured for the clergy in return for food and lodgings. When the city was threatened by foreign invaders the people flocked to the temples.

Nebuchadnezzar's architectural boom included the reconstruction of Sumer and Akkad. But the greatest attention was devoted to the rebuilding of Babylon, a city of 100,000 inhabitants that could accommodate a quarter of a million. The city's ten-mile outer wall was wide enough for two chariots of four horses abreast. Festival Avenue, with a magnificent gate known as Ishtar Gate, led to the palace. Images of lions, made from 3D glazed tiles and symbolic of the goddess Ishtar, kept a watchful eye on passers-by. The palace's roof gardens, the Hanging Gardens of Babylon, are regarded as the seventh wonder of the ancient world. They were built for the king's wife, Amytas, a Mede, so that she would not miss her mountain home. An elaborate irrigation system watered thousands of trees and shrubs brought from every region of the vast empire.

Jeremiah, an Old Testament prophet, called the city 'a golden cup in the Lord's hand that made all the earth drunken'. The Greek historian Herodotus was equally impressed: 'It surpasses in splendour any city of the known world.'

The transformation of Babylon, however, had to be financed. And while the people did not object to living in a magnificent capital, they did not like paying for it. The temples gave up 20% of their revenues, which were also used to pay for the standing army.

Jews in exile

Nebuchadnezzar was a conqueror as well as a builder. The King of Judea gave up without a fight, but lost about 40,000 subjects who were taken captive. The lament 'by the rivers of Babylon, there we sat down yea, we wept, when we remember Zion', still sung in churches today, refers to this period of exile. The Jews were greatly influenced by Babylonian culture and ideas, and legends like that of the flood found their way into the Old Testament. In 538BC, when the armies of Cyrus, the great Persian conqueror, invaded Babylon making it possible for the Jews to return home, many chose to stay. A strong Jewish community developed in Mesopotamia and prospered during

ASSYRIANS TODAY

After the collapse of their massive empire, which lasted for 14 centuries, the Assyrians became a small nation living at the mercy of their overlords in vastly scattered lands in the Middle Eastern region.

They embraced Christianity in the 1st century and today are followers of the ancient church of the East, the Syrian Orthodox Church of Antioch, the Chaldean Catholic Church and various Protestant denominations.

Until the cultural renaissance in the middle of the 19th century, the Assyrians almost lost their identity as a nation when numerous atrocities befell them because of their religious beliefs and origins. Like the Yazedis and Armenians they were the victims of Ottoman massacres. In 1915, the Turks drove them out of the Hokkari mountains where they were living as a semi-independent people under their religious and secular head, Patriarch Mar Shimon, and they joined their brethren in the Urmai and Salams districts of Iran.

The two World Wars proved disastrous as their support was enlisted by the allied forces (British and Russians) at a dreadful cost. In 1918, just before the war ended, they were forced to retreat from Urmia. More than one-third of the population perished during the trek to the British forces in Baghdad. They were settled in camps in Baquba and used to protect the newly installed government of Iraq and British air bases.

Like the Kurds, the Assyrians were promised an independent homeland by the allies. In Iraq they were offered the Mosul district but the promise was not kept. Betrayed by British promises in 1933, 600 were massacred in Simeil and 2,000 in the surrounding villages. A major exodus from Iraq, which is still in evidence today, began.

subsequent centuries of Arab-Islamic rule. The Jews added to the cosmopolitan nature of society where Phoenicians, Syrians and Egyptians exchanged views, partied together and communicated in Aramaic.

Persian conquest

The splendour of Babylon was of no great benefit to the ordinary people who could not make ends meet on their meagre wages. Banking families made a fortune by charging 20–30% interest. As Georges Roux notes in *Ancient Iraq*:

> economic depression contributed to the decline of Mesopotamian civilisation but the temples kept it alive for almost six hundred years. By a remarkable coincidence, this civilisation was to die, as it was born: under the wings of the gods.

Death came slowly in the form of a slow decline and disintegration. It began with the writing on the wall during Belshazzar's feast in 539BC when the king's guests were drinking from cups Nebuchadnezzar had removed from the temple in Jerusalem.

Since 1960 hundreds of Assyrian villages have been destroyed by Iraqi forces in the north of the country. Churches and monasteries have been levelled and the Assyrians have been denied the right to practise their religion and preserve their culture and language. The signing of the 1975 Algiers treaty between Iran and Iraq in 1975 and the attacks on the Kurdish areas in northern Iraq also inhabited by the Assyrians forced hundreds of Assyrians to flee. During the uprising at the end of the Gulf War in 1991 more than 250,000 Assyrians joined the Kurds, who sought refuge in Turkey, Iran and Syria. Some were eventually resettled in Europe, America, Canada and Australia, while others moved to Baghdad and other large cities in Iraq. One of the largest Assyrian communities abroad is in Chicago where, in 1992, they succeeded in getting a stretch of Western Avenue named honorarily after one of their greatest kings, Sargon II (see page 141).

Today reconciliation is in the air in Iraq; churches and monasteries have been rebuilt and rennovated and the Assyrian culture is tolerated. In Mosul and the safe-haven in northern Iraq, the Assyrians have many cultural centres and associations.

The Christian religion is a very important part of Assyrian culture, both in Iraq and among the communites in exile, as it has defined the people for nearly two millennia. The major holiday is Easter, followed by Christmas. The fast of the Ninevites is an ancient religious observance still practised by some, during which all animal products are avoided for three days – the length of time Jonah spent in the whale.

As with all Iraqi people hospitality and visiting are very important among the Assyrians. Music and folk-dancing are part of all festive celebrations.

The *Book of Daniel* tells us:

> In the same hour came forth fingers of a man's hand and wrote over against the candlestick upon the plaister of the wall of the king's palace: and the king saw the part of the hand that wrote.

The Prophet Daniel, one of the Jewish exiles, was asked to interpret the message. He replied:

> God hath numbered thy kingdom and finished it. Thou art weighed in the balances, and art found wanting. Thy kingdom is divided, and given to the Medes and Persians.

While the Babylonians were feasting the armies of Cyrus the Great diverted the waters of the Euphrates into a trench and marched along the dry river bed into the city. For the first time in history the land of the two rivers, the cradle of civilisation, lost its independence and was annexed to a foreign empire. Cyrus proved that empire building could be accomplished with a minimum of destruction. He respected his subjects and life returned to normal along the banks of the Tigris and Euphrates until the power-hungry Xerxes levelled a crippling tax on the people of Babylon to finance his military exploits and tried to replace the Babylonian language with Aramaic. The Persians also monopolised trade with India and the East through the Royal Road from Sardis to Susa which bypassed Babylon. The people revolted and the empire began to crumble. Magnificent buildings were left to decay, the canals silted up and much of the land reverted to desert.

Alexander the Great

In 331BC, Alexander the Great, a pupil of Aristotle, inflicted a series of defeats on the Persians and proposed to make Babylon and Alexandria the twin capitals of his far-flung empire. But his grandiose scheme to make the Euphrates navigable and turn Babylon into a maritime trading centre – linked through trade routes with India and Egypt and by canals between the Red Sea and Nile – was cut short by his death, reportedly of malaria, in Babylon in 323BC.

As its masters changed, Mesopotamian civilisation was dying of old age. In the words of Georges Roux,

> Alexander the Great heralded a new age in which the world was bent
> on extensive commercial intercourse, bursting with curiosity, eager to
> reappraise most of its religious, moral, scientific and artistic values.
> There was no room in such a world for a literature which none but a
> few scholars could read, for an art which drew its inspiration from
> outdated ideals and models, for a science which evaded rational
> explanations, for a religion which did not admit scepticism.

Seleucus, one of Alexander's generals, succeeded him as ruler of Mesopotamia and Persia, then known as the kingdom of the Seleucide, which had its power centre at Seleucia on the Tigris, 20 miles south of modern Baghdad. The Seleucids were challenged by new powers to the north, the Parthian Persians, who competed with the Romans for control of the region. During the Parthian period (126BC–AD227) the city of Hatra was constructed, 80km south of Mosul. The buildings of the 1st and 2nd centuries BC reflected the culture of the conquerors. They accommodated foreign gods, citadels were built on top of old ziggurats and stone replaced mud and brick. Eventually though, the Parthians were pushed aside by a new Persian power, the Sassanian empire (AD227–636), which revived Zoroastrianism, the major Persian religion.

The history of the region then became the history of a series of wars between Western armies and the Persians. Seton Lloyd, author of *Twin Rivers*, describes a long succession of Western armies marching either down the Euphrates or along the Tigris to attack Babylon, Seleucia, Ctesiphon, or whatever city happened at that moment to be the capital of Iraq. One ancient writer speaks of the springtime 'when the kings go forth to war'. For the next 500 years one could almost equally well say 'when kings go up against Mesopotamia'.

By the mid-7th century AD the Sassanids and the Romans were exhausted by their struggles and the Sassanian empire was reduced to a number of small states. The region was ripe for conquest by Arab invaders who had recently converted to Islam, a new monotheistic religion inspired by the teachings of the Prophet Mohammed that were spread by both the book and the sword.

UMAYYADS, ABBASIDS AND OTTOMANS

The invaders from the desert brought with them no tradition of learning, no heritage of culture, to the lands they conquered. In Syria, in Egypt, in Al Iraq, in Persia they sat as pupils at the feet of the people they subdued. But the seed was sown, and the tree of knowledge, which came into full bloom under the early Abbasids in Baghdad, certainly had its roots in the preceding period of Greek, Syrian and Persian Culture.

Philip K Hitti, *History of the Arabs*

Chronology

AD570	Birth of the Prophet Mohammed in Mecca. Emergence of Islam, the third of the monotheistic religions.
632	Death of the Prophet Mohammed in Medina.
661–750	Umayyad caliphs in Damascus. The second caliph (successor to Prophet Mohammed) subjugated Mesopotamia. The time of the greatest expansion of the Muslim empire. Rebellious Arabs were slaughtered in their thousands at Kufa and a series of brutal governors were installed to keep them in a state of subjugation.
750–1258	The Abbasid caliphs in Baghdad. Baghdad replaced Damascus as the capital of the Muslim empire. The golden age of wealth and learning (transmission of Greco-Roman philosophy to the Western world). The rulers promoted medicine, chemistry, geometry, mathematics, astronomy and poetry.
1258–1356	Hulagid Il Khan dynasty. The grandson of Genghis Khan, a great Central Asian conqueror, left behind a trail of horror and destruction.
1356–1410	Jalairid dynasty. The Jalayr kingdom was set up by the family of Amir Hussain Jalayr. They were capable rulers and Baghdad once again became an important town.
1410–1509	Turcoman tribes began gaining influence.
1509–1533	Safawid Persians. Ismail Shah, founder of the Persian Safawid dynasty, conquered Iraq.
1534–1918	Ottoman period. Iraq was divided into three provinces (Baghdad, Mosul and Basrah) by its Turkish rulers. Ottoman rule was characterised by centuries of neglect and poverty. Mosul and Basrah were important commercial centres.

The Umayyads

During the early days of the Islamic conquest Iraq was a province of the Umayyad caliphate with its capital in Damascus. But it soon rose to leadership of the Arab and Islamic world under the Abbasids, whose rule is regarded as the pinnacle of the Islamic past.

> After Prophet Mohammed's death no close series of historical events
> in the Middle East has ever produced results so immediate, yet so
> profound and lasting, as those which followed the unbelievably rapid,
> unexpected and complete conquest by the earliest Muslims, under the
> first successors (or caliphs) of the prophet, of practically all the
> territories of western Asia (except Anatolia) and of north Africa.
> These conquests proved final and irreversible, yet were orderly,
> unmarked by ruin or massacre, and were preliminary not to a violent
> but rather to a peaceful revolution, visible and invisible, in society and
> policies and men's minds throughout the region, and far beyond it.
>
> Stephen Longrigg, *The Middle East, a Social Geography*

The Muslim conquests were successful largely because the people they sought to bring under their control resented the oppression and heavy taxation of their former rulers.

In AD635 the Muslims ended Persian (Sassanid) rule in Iraq at the battle of Qadisiya. The gem-laden banner of the enemy made of panthers' skins was captured. In Ctesiphon the Muslims discovered remarkable treasures but resisted the temptation to attack Persia. The Arab troops, largely nomadic bedouins, were stationed at two military garrisons: Basrah and Kufa. They soon grew into large towns which became the hotbeds of rebellion.

Umayyad society

The Umayyads were responsible for many long-lasting social changes: they changed the caliphate into an empire, they made Arabic the language of the state, minted their own coins and built a number of great mosques including the Dome of the Rock in Jerusalem, the Umayyad mosque in Damascus and the great mosque of Qairawan in present-day Tunisia. The mosques assumed the architectural features of the country: in Syria they were modelled on a square stone watch-tower, whereas in Iraq the mosque took a more traditional Arab form until, at a later date, under the Abassads, the spiral form of minaret originated, inspired by the earlier ziggurats. A regular postal service, schools, hospitals and charities for the sick were also established as was a navy. Basrah became an important port for the Islamic empire, and ships sailed for Sind in Pakistan, East Africa and China. Stories of Sinbad the sailor also became popular at around this time.

Umayyad society was divided into four classes: Arabs, who formed the aristocracy; the neo-Muslims, or converts; the Dhimmis (non–Muslims in an Islamic state – Christians, Jews, Zoroastrians and Berbers); and, finally, slaves.

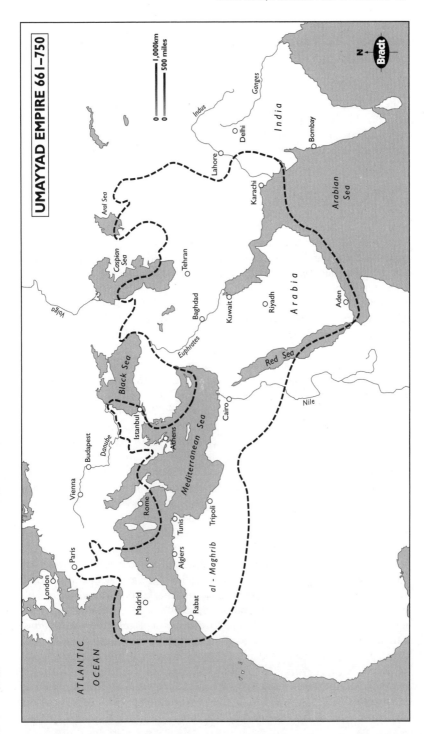

UMAYYAD EMPIRE 661–750

But the Umayyad caliphs never totally abandoned their traditional lifestyle. The young princes were reared in the desert air and royal courts were held in tents. Desert castles and palaces were later built on the favourite camping grounds.

The first Arab empire was a politically, culturally and economically self-contained unit. The world was divided into the House of Islam (*Dar Al Islam*) and the House of War (*Dar Al Harb*). Peace came when the enemies surrendered and converted to Islam. There was little time or need for diplomacy: opponents were quickly subdued and incorporated into the House of Islam.

Conflict and decline

But the Arabs or now Iraqi-Arabs in Basrah and Kufa proved to be a continual thorn in the side of the Ummayad rulers. They resented the fact that Umayyad rule meant Syrian rule, they were excluded from government and treated as non-Arab Muslims (*mawali*), who had to pay higher taxes. They also felt the taxes they paid should be spent to develop the areas from which they were collected. Nor did the local people benefit from the land reclamation projects. Their spiritual allegiance was to Ali, the cousin of the Prophet Mohammed, and they were aggrieved by the events at the battle of Kerbala when Ali's son was killed by the Ummayad ruler Yazid (see pages 229–30).

An attempt was made to rectify the tax status of the Iraqis by Umar bin 'Abd al-Aziz. They were taxed as Muslims who paid only alms (*sadaqa*). But if they sold their land it became the property of the village on which the full land tax (*kharaj*) paid by non-Muslims was levied.

The governors sent to Iraqi areas ruled by a combination of carrot-and-stick and resettlement. Al-Mughira bin Shu'ba Al-Thaqafi, one of Kufa's first governors, converted to Islam, which annulled all past misdeeds, after committing murder. He adopted a policy of benign oversight as long as his authority was not threatened, and allowed the residents to keep the revenues of some districts. On his appointment, Ziyad bin Abihi in Basrah promised that soldiers' salaries (*ata*) would be paid on time and there would be no arduous, distant military campaigns. In AD671 around 50,000 troops were sent to Khurasan as settlers. This temporary 'cure' proved to be worse than the problem: years later these settlers were responsible for bringing down the caliphate itself.

In AD685 Mukhtar bin Abi Ubayd became a prominent political figure. He claimed descent from the Prophet's early followers, was vehemently opposed to Umayyad rule and made himself master of Kufa. He proclaimed one of Ali's descendants, Ibn Al-Hanafiyya, both caliph and *mahdi*, a divine saviour. The idea proved popular and provided the inspiration for future rebellions. Mukhtar was killed during a siege of the governor's palace in 687 but his idea of supporting the downtrodden was readily adopted in the propaganda war against the Umayyads.

One of the most brutal governors was Hajjaj bin Yusuf al-Thaqafi, who was in charge of both Basrah and Kufa. He leapt onto the pulpit (*mimbar*) in Kufa and made a speech famous in Arabic literature:

> People of Kufa, I see that your heads are ripe for cutting. You are
> always making mischief but this time you have made too much of it;
> there must be an end of it. Believe me, an end will be made, and my
> sword will make it.

Some historians claim the massacre resulted in 100,000 deaths.

Internal conflicts plagued the Umayyad dynasty, which alienated many of its former supporters and could not provide the leadership expected of Muslim rulers who became increasing preoccupied with affairs of state. Corruption set in: one of the governors of Iraq was accused of embezzling millions of dirhams.

The Abbasids, descendants of Abbas, the uncle of Prophet Mohammed, appealed to religious legitimacy. They organised themselves into an effective force, which relied heavily on the Persians and Abu-l-Abbas, the great-great grandson of the prophet's uncle, and led a rebellion that toppled the Ummayads in AD750. Abu-l-Abbas called himself the blood-shedder and lived up to his reputation by launching a ruthless extermination campaign against the Umayyads and other popular Abbasid leaders. Arab hegemony over the Islamic empire was brought to an end, the various conquered populations slowly moved up in the social hierarchy and a new society evolved. The Ummayads appealed to the spirit of Arab nationalism but the Abbasids could make no such claim. They sought support from the Muslims of non-Arab origin who had many grievances against the Ummayads and resented being treated as second-class citizens.

The Abbasids
The rise of Islam

For the Abbasids (AD750–1258) Islam was the answer. They were convinced that a divinely guided ruler from the family of the prophet would bring the injustices of the Ummayad era to an end. Emphasis was placed on the equality of all Muslims. Persians played an influential role in the political and cultural life of the empire; appeals to Arab nationalism could no longer be made and descent from an uncle of the prophet helped legitimise the religious credentials of the Abbasids.

But despite the emphasis on equality and an end to discrimination between Arab and non-Arab Muslims, a ruling elite soon developed and the caliph, surrounded by a vast court, lost touch with his subjects and became an absolute ruler, abandoning the traditional Arab notion of a leader chosen by a council of his peers. The palaces were massive institutions with a complex network of servants and secretaries. The door-keeper (hajib) decided who saw the caliph.

The caliph was assisted by the vizier. Muslim judges (qadis) were appointed by the central government. Ministers and senior military officers were in charge of a wage-earning bureaucracy and army. Academics were greatly respected. Next in the pecking order came merchants, farmers, herdsmen and slaves, who ceased to be social outcasts. A magnificent cultural renaissance spanned the reigns of the dynasty's first seven rulers (AD750–842), the most famous being Mansour (AD754–75), Harun al Rashid (AD786–806) and Mamum (AD813–33).

Kufa was the first capital of the Abbasid Empire but Caliph Mansour began the construction of a purpose-built capital, Baghdad, which served as a model for many towns and cities including Cairo. Baghdad soon became the cosmopolitan centre of the medieval world and its richest city, blessed with a plentiful supply of water. The rivers were an important means of communication and there was no malaria. It was a round city with three consecutive enclosures, one for the ruler, surrounded by the army and the people. Caliph Mansour died a few years after the completion of his capital. He ordered that 100 graves were dug for him to ensure that no one could find his tomb and desecrate it.

Harun al Rashid presided over Baghdad in its heyday, established diplomatic relations with Byzantium and sent the Frankish Emperor Charlemagne an elephant as a present. Prosperity, though, led to ridiculous extravagance. When he was forced to seek shelter in a peasant's hut on the Euphrates the bill for lodgings came to 500 dirhams. The caliph inadvertently gave him a warrant on the treasury for 500,000 and insisted this amount was paid. Zubaida, Harun's wife, only allowed vessels of gold or silver studded with gems at her table; Al-Amin, one of Harun's sons, had boats, costing millions of dirhams, made in the shapes of animals. But towards the end of his reign the legendary caliph lost interest in affairs of state and allowed the Barmakid family to exercise power in his name.

Social life centred around parties and hunts, chess, intellectual discussions about literature, philosophy, or religion and poetry and literary symposiums. Outdoor games included polo, fencing, hawking and horse racing. The poet Abu Nawas provided extensive details about court life.

Cultural expansion

Harun divided the empire between his three sons, Amin, Mamum and Qasim, but Amin took the office of caliph. He was soon deposed by Mamum, who was supported by the Persians. Amin tried to escape in a boat

POETRY

The Abbasid period was the heyday of a form of Arab poetry that eulogised those with wealth and power and was given the name 'new poetry'. As in present-day Iraq, poets who pleased their patrons were handsomely rewarded. Muti'b bin Iyas and Abu Nawas were the most famous 'new poets' from the Baghdad school. Abu Nawas advised his patrons to:

> Accumulate as many sins thou canst:
> The Lord is ready to relax His ire.
> When the day comes, forgiveness thou wilt find
> Before a mighty King and gracious Sire,
> And gnaw they fingers, all that joy regretting
> Which thou didst leave thro' terror of Hell–fire!